Scott, Foresman

Science

Series Consultant

Irwin L. Slesnick
Department of Biology
Western Washington University
Bellingham, Washington

Program Consultant

Ronald D. Anderson
Laboratory for Research
in Science and Mathematics Education
University of Colorado
Boulder, Colorado

Reading Consultant

Robert A. Pavlik
Reading-Language Arts Department
Cardinal Stritch College
Milwaukee, Wisconsin

Special Writers

Laboratories
Alfred DeVito
Science Education
Purdue University
Lafayette, Indiana

Enrichment Features
David Newton
Department of Chemistry
Salem State College
Salem, Massachusetts

Authors

Michael R. Cohen
School of Education
Indiana University
Indianapolis, Indiana

Bette J. Del Giorno
Science Consultant
Fairfield Public Schools
Fairfield, Connecticut

Jean Durgin Harlan
Education Division
University of Wisconsin, Parkside
Kenosha, Wisconsin

Alan J. McCormack
Science and Mathematics
Teaching Center
College of Education
University of Wyoming
Laramie, Wyoming

John R. Staver
College of Education and
College of Liberal Arts and Sciences
University of Illinois at Chicago
Chicago, Illinois

Cover: Northern cricket frogs are found in the eastern and central United States. They live at the edges of swamps, ponds, and streams.

Scott, Foresman and Company

Editorial Offices: Glenview, Illinois

Regional Offices: Palo Alto, California
Tucker, Georgia • Glenview, Illinois
Oakland, New Jersey • Dallas, Texas

Reviewers and Contributors

Gretchen M. Alexander
Program Coordinator
Museum of Science and Industry
Chicago, Illinois

Daniel W. Ball
Division of Education
Northeast Missouri State University
Kirksville, Missouri

Mary Coban
Teacher
Divine Savior School
Norridge, Illinois

Thomas Graika
Science Chairman
School District 102
LaGrange, Illinois

Robert G. Guy
Science Teacher
Big Lake Elementary School
Sedro Woolley, Washington

Irma G. Hamilton
Science Teacher
Oglethorpe Elementary School
Atlanta, Georgia

Judy Haney
Teacher
East Noble School Corporation
Kendallville, Indiana

Garth P. Harris
Teacher
Lincoln Elementary School
Evanston, Illinois

Edwina Hill
Principal
Oglethorpe Elementary School
Atlanta, Georgia

LaVerne Jackson, Sr.
Science Teacher
Medgar Evers Elementary School
Chicago, Illinois

Hollis R. Johnson
Astronomy Department
Indiana University
Bloomington, Indiana

Irene S. Kantner
Teacher
Lincoln Elementary School
Evanston, Illinois

Sol Krasner
Department of Physics
University of Chicago
Chicago, Illinois

Dolores Mann
Teacher
Glenview Public Schools
Glenview, Illinois

Phillip T. Miyazawa
Instructional Consultant
Science Education
Denver Public Schools
Denver, Colorado

Anita E. Moore
Principal
George Howland Elementary School
Chicago, Illinois

Janet Ostrander
Teacher
Indian Trail School
Highland Park, Illinois

Barbara Scott
Teacher
Crown Magnet School
Chicago, Illinois

Elaine R. Seaman
Teacher
Greenbrier Elementary School
Arlington Heights, Illinois

R. A. Slotter
Department of Chemistry
Northwestern University
Evanston, Illinois

Anita Snell
Coordinator of Primary Education
Spring Branch Independent
School District
Houston, Texas

Lois Spangler
Teacher
Central School
Great Meadows, New Jersey

Carol Leth Stone
Biology Writer
Stanford, California

Johanna F. Strange
Model Laboratory School
Eastern Kentucky University
Richmond, Kentucky

William D. Thomas
Science Supervisor
Escambia County Schools
Pensacola, Florida

Dorothy Wallinga
Christian Schools International
Grand Rapids, Michigan

Les Wallinga
Science Teacher
Calvin Christian Junior High School
Wyoming, Michigan

12345678910 RRC 9291908988878685

When You Read This Book

1 Read the question.

2 Look at the pictures.

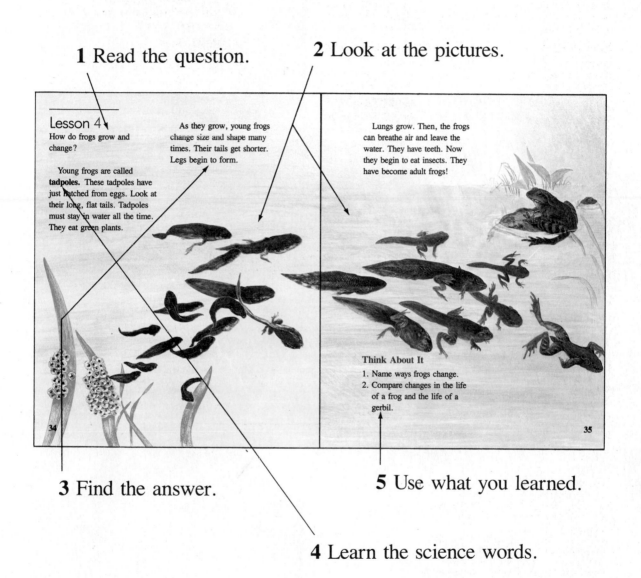

Lesson 4

How do frogs grow and change?

Young frogs are called **tadpoles.** These tadpoles have just hatched from eggs. Look at their long, flat tails. Tadpoles must stay in water all the time. They eat green plants.

As they grow, young frogs change size and shape many times. Their tails get shorter. Legs begin to form.

Lungs grow. Then, the frogs can breathe air and leave the water. They have teeth. Now they begin to eat insects. They have become adult frogs!

Think About It

1. Name ways frogs change.
2. Compare changes in the life of a frog and the life of a gerbil.

34

35

3 Find the answer.

5 Use what you learned.

4 Learn the science words.

UNIT ONE Your Body

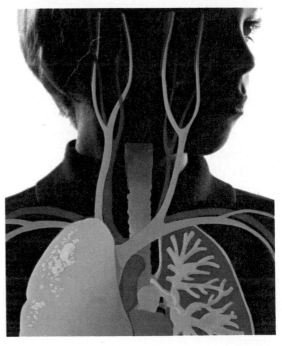

UNIT TWO Animals

UNIT THREE Matter

UNIT FOUR Heat

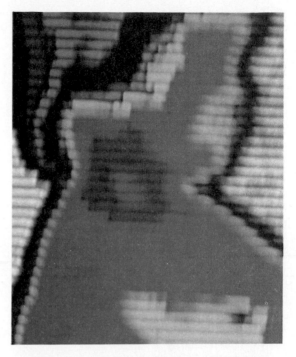

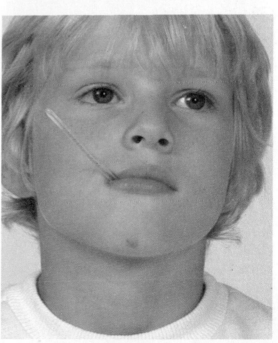

UNIT FIVE Motion

UNIT SIX A Trip into Space

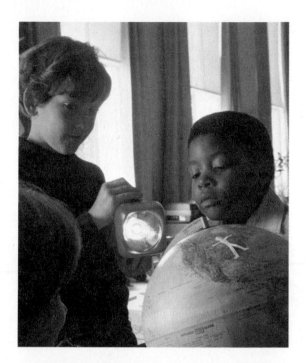

UNIT SEVEN Plants

UNIT EIGHT Habitats and Homes

UNIT ONE
YOUR BODY

Change happens.
Sometimes slowly
Sometimes quickly
But everybody changes
Sometimes.

Be Singer *age 8*

3

Chapter 1
A Special
Person . . . You!

Lesson 1

Collect some
fingerprints.

Your fingerprints are special. No one else
has fingerprints just like yours.

Think About It

Which of these prints show the same
finger?

5

Lesson 2

How are we different?

Observe this girl. When you observe, you look carefully. Look at the color of the girl's hair. Look at her eyes. Look at the shape of her face.

Now find the girl in her class. No other child is just the same. Each person is special.

Think About It

Name ways these children are different from one another.

Lesson 3
How will you change?

You are growing. Your shape and size are changing. You can **measure** how tall you are. Next year, you may be taller.

Sometimes you will grow fast. Other times you will grow slowly. As you change, you become special in new ways.

Think About It

1. Name ways you might change.
2. Name ways you might stay the same.

Activity

Measure parts of your body.

Step 1 Stretch some string along your arm.

Step 2 Mark the string to show how long your arm is. Cut the string where you marked it.

Step 3 Measure other parts of your body.

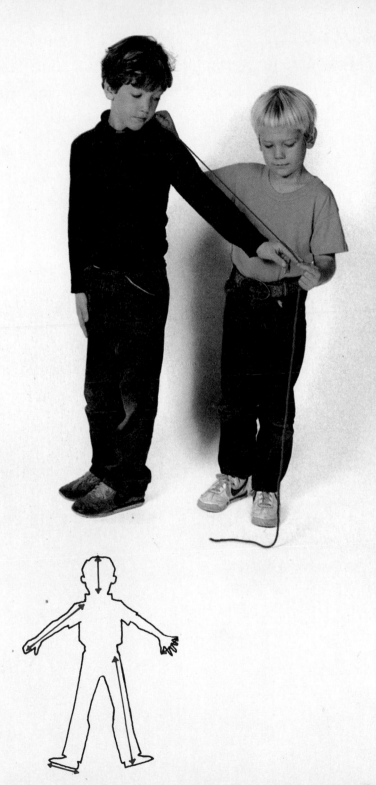

Think About It

1. Which part is the longest?
2. Which part do you think will grow the most?

Do You Know...

Some Body Parts
Grow More Than
Others!

Look at the
baby's head. See
how it will grow
and change.

Look at the
baby's legs. See
how they will
grow and change.

A child's head is
almost full-grown
in seven years.
Other body parts
can keep growing
for twenty years!

Tie It Together

1. Draw a person.

2. Tell how the person is special.

3. Tell how the person might grow and change.

Science Words
measure
observe

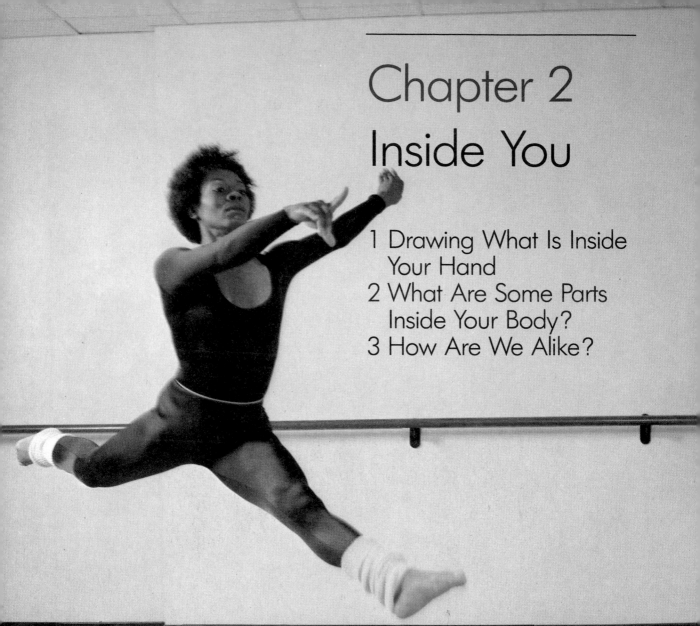

Chapter 2
Inside You

Lesson 1

Draw what is inside your hand.

First, outline your hand on paper. Next, wiggle your fingers. Look at both sides of your hand as your fingers move. Look at your wrist. Feel the parts moving inside as you open and close your hand.

Now, draw what you think is inside your hand.

Think About It

What do you think happens inside your hand when it grows?

Lesson 2

What are some parts inside your body?

Your body has many **bones.** The bones help give your body its shape. Your bones fit together at **joints.**

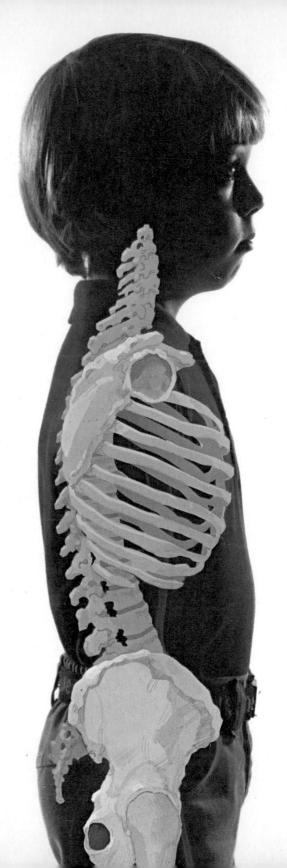

Your bones move
because you
have **muscles** to
pull them. The
muscles are attached
to your bones.

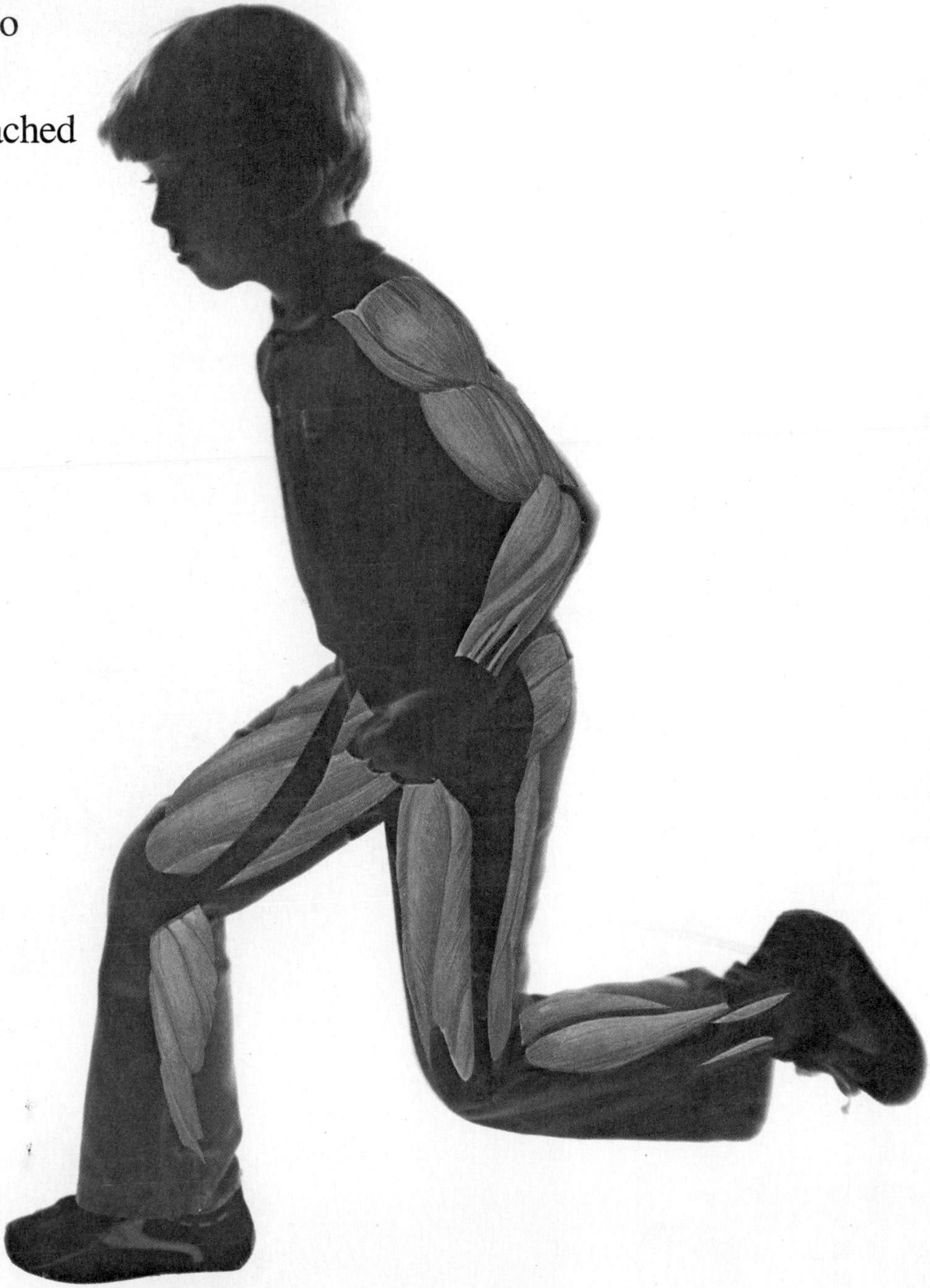

What body parts are always working?

Air goes to your **lungs** and a part of it mixes with your **blood.** Your **heart** pumps the blood to all parts of your body.

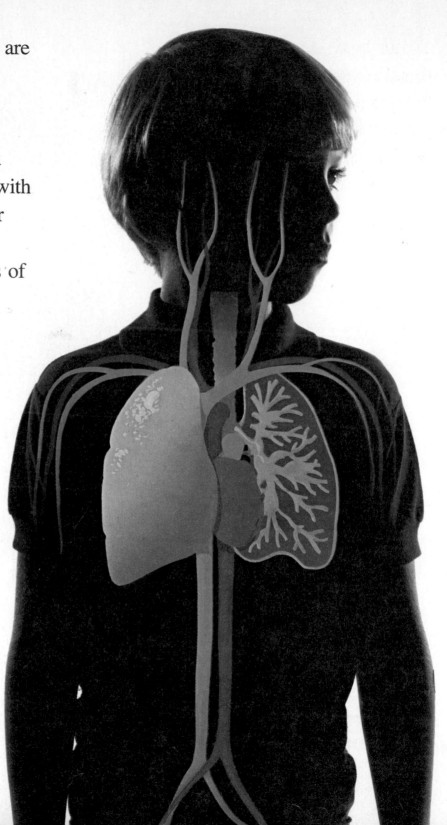

The food you swallow goes through a tube to your **stomach.** Then juices in your stomach work to break down the food.

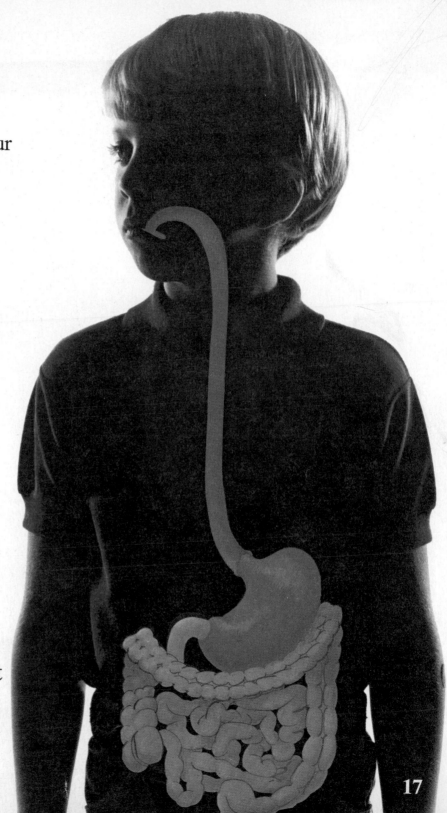

Think About It

Name some parts inside your body.

17

Do You Know...

How Does Food Get to All the Parts of Your Body?

Inside your stomach, food changes. It breaks down into parts too tiny to see. The food you eat becomes a liquid.

The liquid food in your stomach mixes with your blood. Your blood carries the food to all parts of your body.

Activity

Count your heartbeats.

Every time your heart beats, it pumps blood through your body. You can feel the blood moving inside your neck.

Step 1 Look at the person in the picture. Put your fingers in the same place on your own neck.

Step 2 Count ten beats while you are sitting still.

Step 3 Do an exercise twenty times. Count ten beats again.

Think About It

When did you have to count faster?

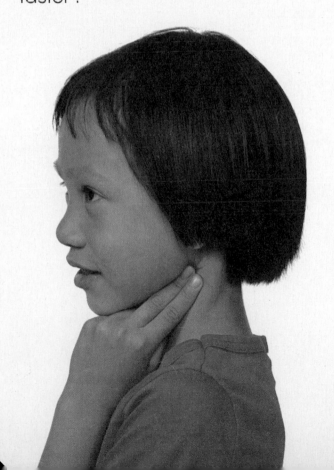

Lesson 3
How are we alike?

We all need food.
These foods help
our bodies stay
healthy.

We all need
exercise. Muscles
work best when we
use them often.

We all need
sleep. Our bodies
feel better when we
get enough rest.

21

What can help our bodies work well?

Food, exercise, and rest all help keep our bodies healthy. Our bodies work best when we are also happy with ourselves.

Sometimes other people can help. We like to have others care about us.

Think About It

Name ways people are alike.

22

Tie It Together

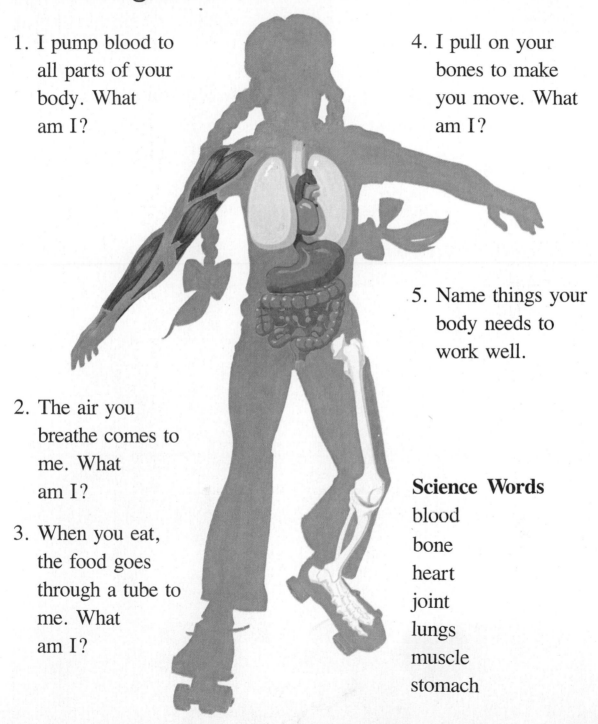

1. I pump blood to all parts of your body. What am I?

2. The air you breathe comes to me. What am I?

3. When you eat, the food goes through a tube to me. What am I?

4. I pull on your bones to make you move. What am I?

5. Name things your body needs to work well.

Science Words
blood
bone
heart
joint
lungs
muscle
stomach

Careers
Dancers

Dancers learn to do twists, turns, and leaps that look almost impossible!

Becoming a dancer takes many years of training. The first thing dancers learn is how to warm up their muscles. Special exercises help them stretch almost all the muscles in their bodies.

Dancers practice for hours and hours. Then their bodies can bend and twist in new ways.

24

On Your Own

1. Look at an old picture of yourself. Tell how you have changed.

2. Ask someone to trace your body on paper. Draw some parts of your body inside.

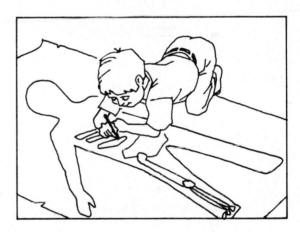

3. Pick an exercise you like to do. Try doing the excrcise ten times each day for a week.

UNIT TWO
ANIMALS

Animals in the
   jungle
Animals in the
   zoo
Animals almost
   anywhere
And some of them
   are new.

Teresa Holloway *age 7*

Chapter 3
Growing and Changing

Lesson 1

Compare these young animals with their parents.

Think About It

1. Which young animals will change the most?
2. Draw a picture of how these young birds might change.

Lesson 2
How do young
animals look?

Young animals
are much smaller
than their parents.
After the young are
born, they grow and
change.

Some animals grow inside eggs their mothers **lay.** When the young get big enough, they **hatch** out of the eggs.

The young will grow more. They will become **adult** animals that look like their parents.

Think About It

1. Describe some young animals.
2. Tell how the young animals will change.

Lesson 3

How do gerbils grow and change?

A mother gerbil has many young at one time. The young gerbils have no hair when they are born. Their eyes are still closed. The young get milk from their mother. The milk helps them grow.

Young gerbils are born with the same shape as adult gerbils. After just one week, they have hair. In about three weeks, their eyes open. They can eat solid food. They can run fast.

Think About It

1. Name three ways young gerbils change.
2. Name one way they stay the same.

Do You Know...

How Fast Do Young Animals Grow Up?

In just three weeks, gerbils can leave their parents.

Turtles are on their own as soon as they hatch from the eggs.

Young chimpanzees stay with their mothers for six years.

A fly is an adult when it is two weeks old. Then it can lay eggs.

Some kinds of animals become adults sooner than other kinds.

Lesson 4

How do frogs grow and change?

Young frogs are called **tadpoles.** These tadpoles have just hatched from eggs. Look at their long, flat tails. Tadpoles must stay in water all the time. They eat green plants.

As they grow, young frogs change size and shape many times. Their tails get shorter. Legs begin to form.

Lungs grow. Then, the frogs can breathe air and leave the water. They have teeth. Now they begin to eat insects. They have become adult frogs!

Think About It

1. Name ways frogs change.
2. Compare changes in the life of a frog and the life of a gerbil.

Activity

Look for these changes as a mealworm grows.

Mealworms are not really worms! They are insects. They start as eggs too tiny to see. They grow up to become black beetles.

2. about five months old

1. about two months old

Think About It

How many different shapes does a mealworm have as it grows?

3. adult

Tie It Together

1. Which animals look like their parents?

2. Which animals hatch from eggs?

3. Which animals change shape as they grow?

Science Words

adult   lay
compare   tadpole
hatch

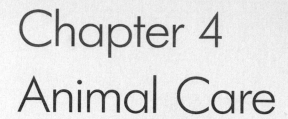

Chapter 4
Animal Care

Lesson 1

Tell how to care for a pet.

Think About It

1. Name what the pet needs.
2. Show how you would care for this pet.

39

Lesson 2

How do animals care for their young?

Think About It

Tell what these adults are doing
for their young.

Do You Know ...

Baby Kangaroos Live in Pockets!

A kangaroo baby is called a *joey.* When the joey is born, it is the size of your thumb. Right away, the joey crawls into its mother's pouch.

For the first months, the joey stays in the pouch all the time. The pouch has plenty of milk to help the joey grow.

Later, the joey explores outside the pouch. But when the joey is tired or scared, it hops right back into the pouch.

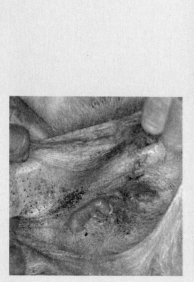

Lesson 3

Do all young animals need care?

These young animals get very little care from adult animals. They care for themselves as soon as they hatch.

Think About It

Compare the needs of kittens and snails.

Activity

Make a pet care chart.

Step 1 Choose a pet. Write what it needs across the top of your chart.

Step 2 Write the days of the week along the side of your chart.

Step 3 Put X's in the boxes to show the care you would give your pet each day.

Think About It

1. Name pets that need a lot of care.
2. Name pets that need very little care.

	food	water	cleanup
Sun.			
Mon.			
Tues.			
Wed.			
Thurs.			
Fri.			
Sat.			

44

Tie It Together

1. When I hatch from my egg, I am ready to be on my own. What am I?

2. I need a lot of care when I am first born. The adults watch for danger and keep me safe. What am I?

3. I make a good pet. My owner feeds me and keeps my bottle full of water. I get exercise by running on my wheel. What am I?

45

Careers
Zoo Keepers

Imagine taking care of an elephant or a giraffe. Large animals need many of the same things that pets need. But they need a lot more space and a lot more food!

Zoo keepers care for the zoo animals. They help plan the space, the food, and the exercise the animals will get.

On Your Own

1. Make cards with pictures of young animals. Make more cards with pictures of the adult animals. Write the names of the animals on the backs of the cards. See if your friends can match the young animals with their parents.

2. Think of an animal you want to know more about. Find out about that animal at your school or town library.

3. Watch a television show about animals. Report to the class three things you learned from the show.

UNIT THREE
MATTER

Hands,
Some kind of clay,
Water,
Mix and turn into mud.
Finally—a pot.

Annie Antone *age 7*

Chapter 5
Solids, Liquids, and Gases

1 Making a Collection
2 What Is Matter?
3 How Does Matter Change?

Lesson 1

Make a collection.

Find a container. Collect anything that will fit inside. Fill as much space as you can.

Choose one thing from your collection. Tell how it feels. Name its colors. Tell about its shape.

When you describe something, you name its **properties.**

Think About It

1. Name the properties of something else in your collection.
2. What is in your container when it looks empty?

Lesson 2

What is **matter**? Matter is
anything that takes up space!

These **solids** are matter.
Solids take up space and have
shapes of their own.

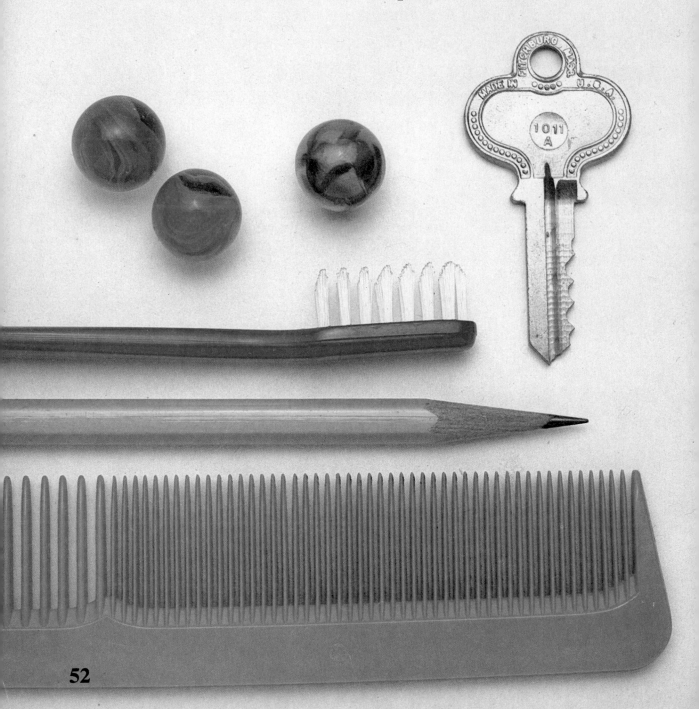

These **liquids** are matter. Liquids take up space, but they have no shape of their own. Liquids **flow.** When you pour a liquid, it changes shape to fill the space in the container.

Can you always see matter?

Gases are matter. They take up space, but they have no shape. Gases spread out to fill their containers. Many gases are **invisible**—you cannot see them.

Air is made of invisible gases. These toys have air inside.

Think About it

1. Which of the toys has the least air?
2. Name a solid, a liquid, and a gas.

Activity

Make a gas.

Step 1 Put vinegar in a bottle.

Step 2 Put baking soda in a bag.

Step 3 Tie the bag over the top of the bottle.

Step 4. Lift the bag. Watch what happens when the vinegar and soda mix!

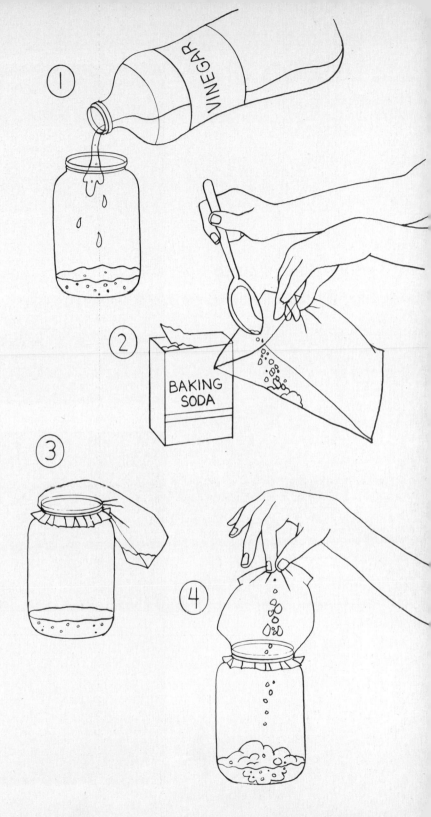

Think About It

1. Name the liquid.
2. Name the solid.
3. What space did the gas fill?

Lesson 3

How does matter change?

Solids can change
to liquids.

Liquids can change
to gases.

Liquids can change
to solids.

Think About It

1. Name the solids, liquids,
   and gases in the pictures.
2. Describe how they are
   changing.

Imagine ...
Oobleck Is Falling!

Describe this sticky green matter. What are its properties?

Is it a liquid? Is it a solid? Do you think it is changing?

How could this strange matter be used? Perhaps as a glue or a paint?

What would YOU do with oobleck?

Tie It Together

1. Name all the solids, liquids, and gases in this picture.

2. Choose something in the picture, and list its properties. Describe how it could change.

Science Words

flow   matter

gas   property

invisible   solid

liquid

59

Chapter 6
Investigating Matter

Lesson 1

Find some properties of a noodle. How does it feel? What color is it? Does it have a shape?

You can learn more by doing things to the noodle. In this way, you **investigate** to find out more properties.

Put the noodle in water. Can you make it stay on top of the water? Can you make it sink?

Try to bend the noodle. What happens if it soaks in hot water?

Think About It

List five properties of a noodle.

Lesson 2

What bends and what breaks?

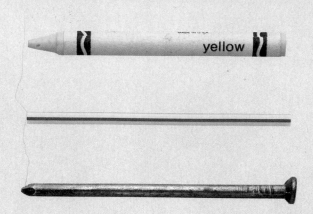

You cannot know if
something will bend by just
looking at it. You must test the
object to find out.

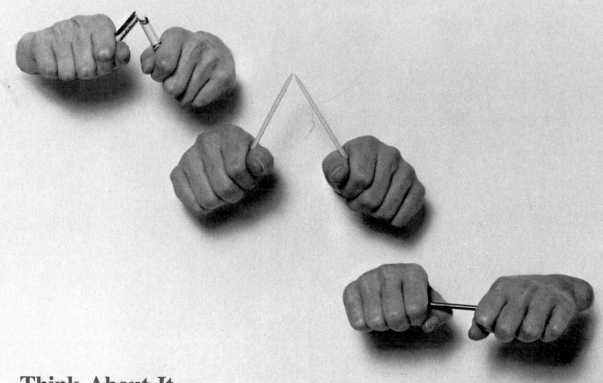

Think About It

1. List some objects that bend.
2. List some objects that break.

Lesson 3

What floats and what sinks?

Name some toys you like to play with in the water. Tell which toys float and which toys sink.

Some objects in the picture will float, and some will sink. Compare them with the toys you know. Tell if you think the objects in the picture will float or sink. You **predict** when you say what you think will happen.

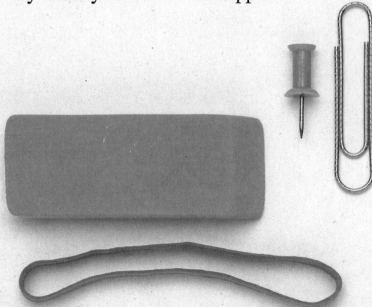

Did you predict what
happened?

Find some objects, and
investigate on your own.

Think About It

1. List some objects that float.
2. List some objects that sink.

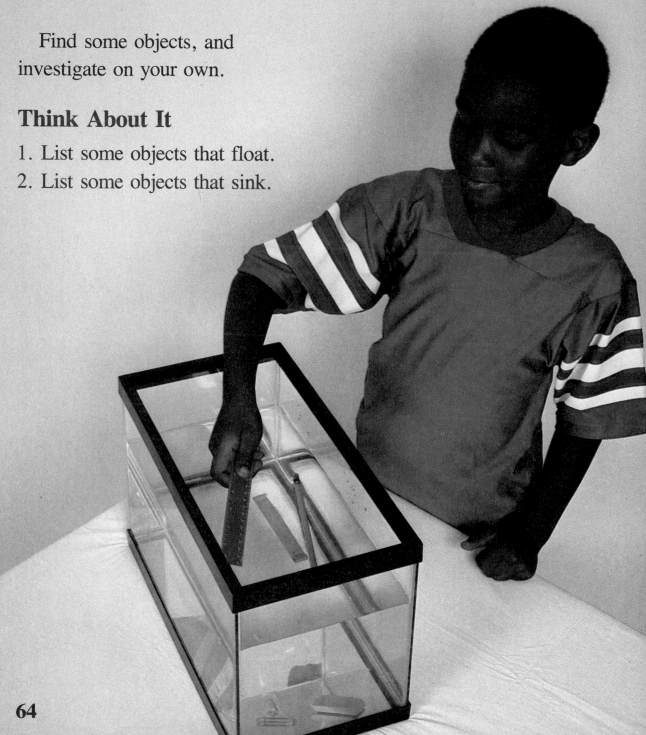

Do You Know...

Liquids Can Float!

Oil does not mix well with vinegar. Even if you shake them up together, they will separate into two layers.

The oil floats on top of the vinegar!

Activity

Find out which matter will mix with water.

Step 1 Place drops of water on waxed paper. Then try mixing tiny amounts of different matter with each drop of water.

Step 2 Watch what happens to each kind of matter. Tell what you observe.

Step 3 Now predict what will happen if you mix salt with water. Investigate, and tell what you observe.

Think About It

1. Which matter mixed with water?
2. Which matter can you take back out of the water?

Tie It Together

1. Name three properties of this ball.

2. Name three properties of this bolt.

Science Words

investigate

predict

Careers

Potters

Some people spin clay on a potter's wheel to make bowls and other objects. Spinning the clay while pushing on it helps give it an even shape.

The potter must also squeeze out air bubbles that get in clay when it is mixed with water. Air bubbles can ruin pottery.

After the clay is shaped, it is baked in an oven. Baking takes the liquid out of the clay and makes it hard. Then the pot is ready to use!

On Your Own

1. Put an ice cube in a dish. Watch it melt. Find out how long it takes to change from solid to liquid to gas.

2. Collect solid objects you can soak in water. Predict how they might change. Investigate to find out!

3. Put food coloring in different liquids such as milk, water, and oil. Compare how they mix.

UNIT FOUR
HEAT

The firefighter
   is busy
Fighting fire
   with a hose
Helping people out

Juleanne Birdd *age 7*

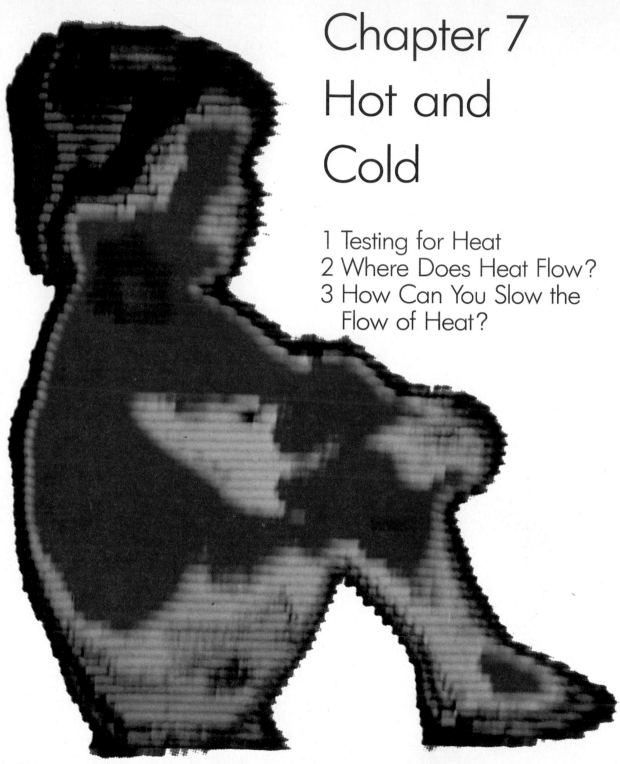

Chapter 7
Hot and Cold

Lesson 1

Test for heat.

Place a metal object on your cheek. Does it feel warm or cool?

Next, hold the object tightly in your hand while you count to 100.

Now, place the object on your cheek again. Describe any changes you feel.

Think About It

1. Which time did the metal object feel warmer?
2. Where did the extra heat come from?

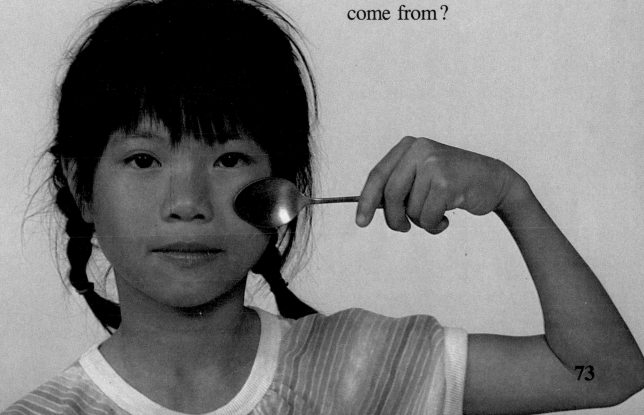

Lesson 2
Where does heat flow?

Can you remember jumping into a cool pool of water? Some heat from your body flowed into the cooler water. The water became warmer while your skin cooled off.

Heat usually flows from hotter places to colder places. When you take a hot bath, heat from the water flows into your body. The heat makes your skin feel warmer. The bath water gets cool as the heat flows out of it.

Think About It

Describe where heat flows when you make toast.

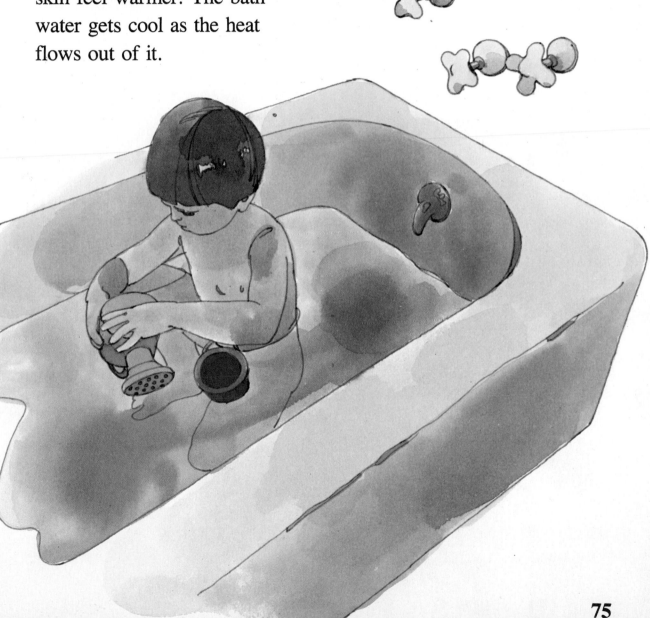

Lesson 3

How can you slow the flow of heat?

When you touch a cold metal bar at recess, heat from your body warms it up. Your hand feels cold as your heat flows into the metal.

Mittens can keep heat in your hands from flowing out so quickly. On very cold days, you might cover yourself with a coat, a hat, mittens, and boots. These clothes trap the warm air and keep it close to your body.

Think About It
What clothing should you wear outside today?

Do You Know ...

How Do Birds Stay Warm in Winter?

Birds have many kinds of feathers. Tail and wing feathers help a bird fly.

The feathers next to a bird's skin—down feathers—are soft and fluffy. They keep the bird warm.

The bird's body heat goes into the air. Down feathers trap that warm air and keep it close to the bird's body.

A bird can move its feathers to let the heated air out.

Activity

Make coats for ice cubes!

Heat in the air can flow into an ice cube and melt it. You wear a coat to keep your body heat in. But the ice cube needs something to keep heat out.

Step 1 Get ice cubes of the same size. Get some foil, paper, cotton, and cloth.

Step 2 Wrap up some ice cubes. Leave one cube unwrapped.

Step 3 Unwrap the cubes after one hour. Compare their sizes and shapes.

Think About It

1. Which cube melted the most?
2. Which cube melted the least?
3. Which material keeps heat out best?

Tie It Together

1. Find objects with a lot of heat.

2. Find objects with very little heat.

3. Tell where some of the heat is flowing.

4. Find something that slows the flow of heat.

Chapter 8
Temperature

1 Observing Hot and
Cold by Touching
2 Can We Measure How
Hot Something Is?

Lesson 1

Observe hot and cold by touching.

Fill three bowls with water.

First, put both hands in Bowl 2. Describe how the water feels to your hands.

Next, put one hand in Bowl 1 and the other hand in Bowl 3. Keep them in the water while you count to 20.

Now, put both hands back in Bowl 2. Describe how the water feels this time!

Think About It

Did the water change or did your skin change?

Use water as hot as you can touch.

Use water that feels the same as your skin—not hot and not cold.

Use water that feels very cold.

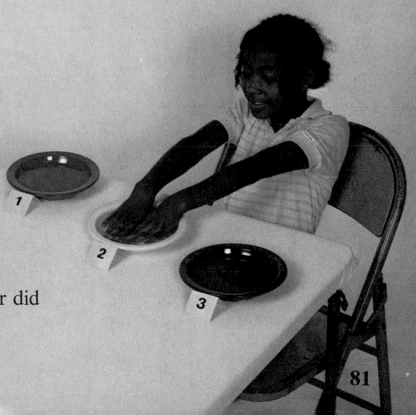

Lesson 2

Can we measure
how hot something
is?

You can feel
some matter to find
out if it is hot or
cold. But you might
be fooled! Things
can feel different
when your fingers
are already hot or
cold.

Use a **thermometer**
to measure exactly
how hot something
is.

All thermometers
have numbers to read.
The numbers show
the **temperature.**
Temperature is a
measure of exactly
how hot something is.

Some thermometers are in the kitchen. They measure the temperature of food.

Thermometers measure the temperature of air.

A thermometer can measure the temperature of your body.

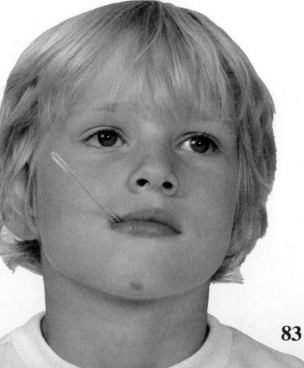

How does a thermometer work?

Most thermometers have a liquid inside. When this liquid is cold, it does not take up much space.

The end of the liquid is near a smaller number when the temperature is low.

The liquid heats up if you place the thermometer near something warm. As the liquid gets warm it **expands**—or takes up more space.

The end of the liquid is near a larger number when the temperature is higher.

Think About It

Which thermometer shows the warmest temperature?

Activity

Measure some temperatures.

Step 1 Get a thermometer. Measure the temperature of cold water. Measure the temperature of your hand.

Step 2 Measure the temperature of the air inside and outside your school.

Step 3 Record as many different temperatures as you can.

Think About It

1. What is the highest temperature you found?
2. What is the lowest temperature you found?

Do You Know . . .
Food Helps Keep You Warm!

Your body uses most of the food you eat to keep your temperature at 37 degrees.

When you shiver in the cold, your body is working to warm you up.

When you sweat in the heat, your body is very busy cooling you down. The sweat helps you get rid of extra heat.

When you wear the right clothes for the weather, your body does not have to work as hard.

Tie It Together

1. You can feel if something is warm or cool. But to measure the exact temperature, you use a _____.

2. As the liquid in a thermometer gets warmer, it _____.

3. You read the numbers on a thermometer to find the _____.

4. What is the temperature on the thermometer in the picture?

Science Words
expand
temperature
thermometer

Careers
Heating Engineers

Many buildings need heat when the weather turns cold. A heating engineer works to make sure that all rooms will be the right temperature.

Air in the furnace gets warm and then moves through ducts. The man in the picture is using a thermometer to find the air temperature in the duct. This air will go into all the rooms in the house.

Furnaces can keep us warm even when it is cold outside.

On Your Own

1. Find out how your family keeps food warm.

2. Measure the temperature outside every day for two weeks. Do it at the same time each day. Make a chart and record the temperatures.

3. Fill a plastic foam cup and a metal cup with the same amount of warm water. Measure the temperature of the water every five minutes. Compare how fast the water cools.

UNIT FIVE
MOTION

A basketball
player is
reaching for
baskets.
Will she win?

Adrienne Freed *age 10*

Chapter 9
Motion and Friction

right

left

92

Lesson 1

Meet Lily and her pet frog, Pad. You can observe where they move.

Make your own puppets. Draw Lily and Pad on cardboard. Cut them out. Make Lily stand up at the middle of your desk.

Place Pad to Lily's left and then to her right. Help Pad hop in front of Lily, above her, and behind her.

Next, make a chain of ten paper clips to measure how far away Pad hops. Help Pad hop to a place 3 paper clips in front of Lily. Help Pad hop to a place 5 paper clips behind Lily.

Now find a place for Pad to rest.

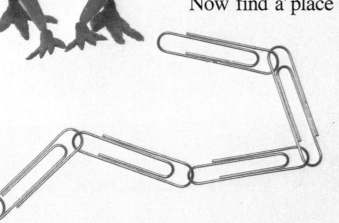

Think About It

Tell how Lily would describe where Pad is resting.

Lesson 2

How can you tell when something moves?

Pad moves around all the time. When Pad is changing places, we say he is in **motion.** Pad moves by hopping.

Lily took pictures of Pad in motion. Here are pictures of Pad hopping from a place far away to a place nearby.

Here are pictures
of Pad hopping
along the road.

As Pad moves,
he comes closer to
some objects and
goes farther away
from other objects.

Think About It

1. Why does Pad look so small
   in some pictures?
2. Name things in the pictures
   that did not move.

Lesson 3

What holds back motion?

Lily is giving Pad a ride. They cannot go fast. The box will not slide.

The box rubs against the ground. The rubbing causes **friction** between the box and the ground. Friction makes it hard to slide objects.

Sometimes Lily does not want to slide. Friction helps keep her from slipping.

Think About It

Where would you put the box to help Lily slide it?

Imagine ...
Being Stuck on the Ice!

Every time Lily moves, her feet slip and slide. It seems as if there is no friction at all.

Think of ways Lily can get to the edge of the ice.

Activity

Make some motion paths.
  Pad moves in many directions. His paths have different shapes.

Step 1 Make your puppet hop, swim, and jump up and down.

Step 2 Now help Pad follow these motion paths.

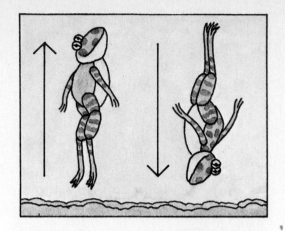

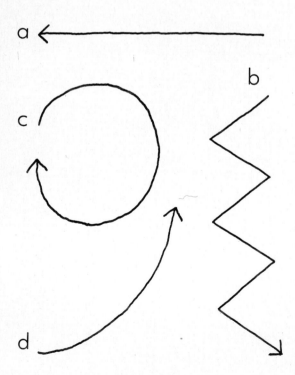

a

b

c

d

Think About It

1. Draw the path you would make on a swing.
2. Draw the path you would make on a roller coaster.

Tie It Together

Tell Pad how to find Lily.

Science Words
friction
motion

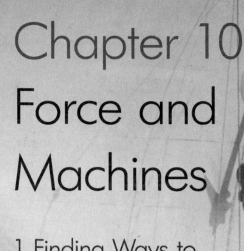

Chapter 10

Force and Machines

Lesson 1

Find ways to move a can.

Work with a group. Think of many different ways to move the can.

Think of ways to use other objects to move the can.

Think of ways to move the can without touching it.

First, list your ideas. Then, try them to see if they work!

Think About It

1. Tell what pushed or pulled the can.
2. Tell how you could stop a can that is moving.

Lesson 2

What makes objects move?

Objects do not start moving by themselves. You must use **force** to make an object start moving. A force is a push or a pull.

You can get light objects moving with just a little force.

You need more force to get heavy objects moving.

What are ways we use force?

When you push or pull, you use force. More force makes objects move faster.

A force can stop moving objects.

Think About It

Name things you push and things you pull.

Activity
Compare forces.

Step 1 Make a hole in the side of a box. Tie a rubber band through the hole.

Step 2 Put objects in the box. Pull on the rubber band until the box begins to move. Use a ruler to measure how far the rubber band stretched.

Step 3 Put other objects in the box. Make the box move slowly. Make the box move fast. Measure the rubber band. Compare how far it stretched each time.

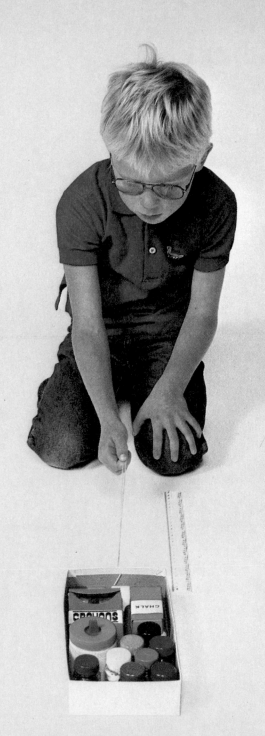

Think About It
1. Tell which time you used the most force.
2. Tell which time you used the least force.

Lesson 3

How do **machines** help you?

A machine helps you do a job faster and easier. With machines, you need less force to start objects moving.

Some machines have many parts.

106

Other machines are very simple.

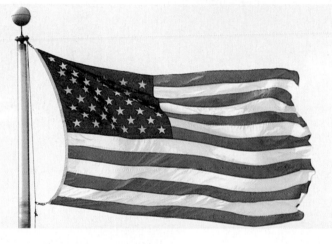

Think About It

1. Explain how you could move a big box.
2. Name some machines in your home.

Do You Know ...
The Earth Pulls on You!

When you jump high, you do not float out to space. When you throw a ball into the air, it soon falls back to the ground.

A big force pulls you and the earth together. The force is called gravity. It pulls on everything.

Gravity holds the dishes on the table. It makes water stay in the bottom of a glass. Gravity makes the rain fall down—not up.

Your life would be very different without gravity.

Tie It Together

1. Which objects are moving?

2. Where does the force come from?

3. What machines can you find?

Science Words
force
machine

Careers
Skaters

Skaters spend a lot of time in motion. They make many paths on the ice—straight paths, curved paths, even figure eights!

On smooth ice, a skater does not need much force to get moving. More force makes the skater go faster.

Some skaters play ice hockey. There is almost no friction as the puck whizzes along. A slapshot can send the puck right into the net. The whole team cheers when they make a goal.

On Your Own

1. Make up a story about Lily and Pad. Have them move in many ways. Use your puppets to act out the story.

2. Play tag with some friends. First, run only in straight paths. Next, use only curved paths.

3. Go on a machine hunt at home. Find as many different machines as you can.

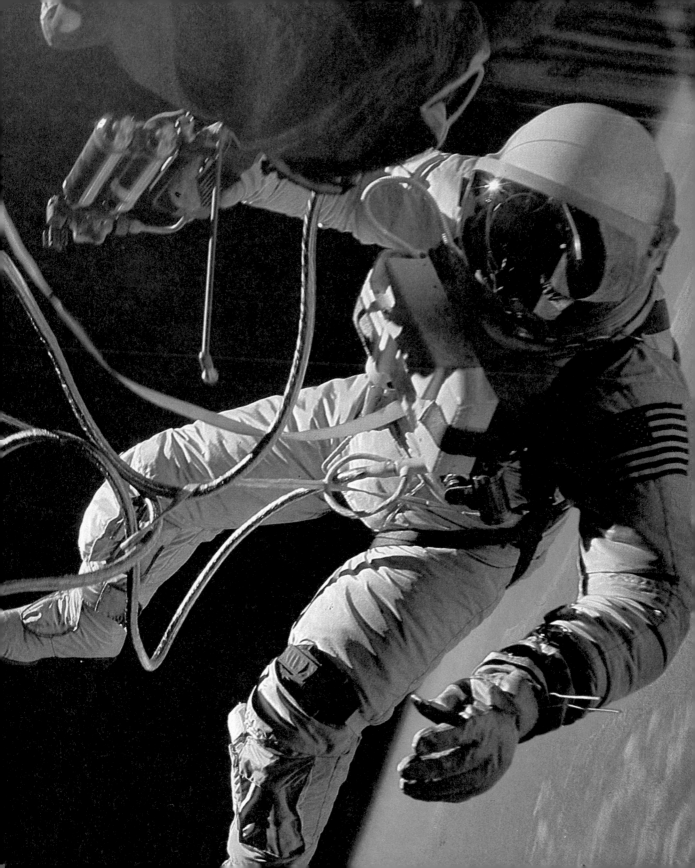

UNIT SIX
A TRIP INTO SPACE

Wears a helmet
   and suit
Goes into space
   and is happy
   he can float.
Spaceman.

Noland Johnson *age 8*

Chapter 11
Earth and Sun

Lesson 1

Make a **model** spaceship.

We are getting ready for a trip into space. You can make a model spaceship from cardboard. A model is a copy of something real.

Hop aboard. Fasten your seatbelt. We are ready to blast off!

Think About It

What should you take on your trip?

Lesson 2

What shape is the earth?

Our spaceship is blasting off. Look out the window as we move away from the ground.

Everything looks so small!

Wow! We are above the clouds!

The edge of the earth is curved!

Now we can see the earth from space. It is round, like a giant ball. We can see the earth's land and water. We can see clouds in the earth's air.

Think About It

Where do you think people live on the earth?

Lesson 3

How does the earth move?

Changes take place as we watch the earth.

In a few hours, we see different shapes of land.

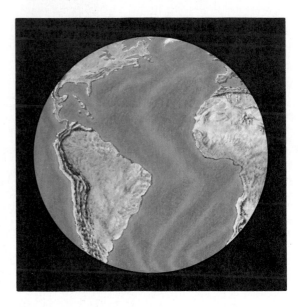

The earth is spinning! It takes 24 hours—one whole day—for the earth to spin around one time.

The earth also moves around the sun. The trip around the sun takes one whole year. We call the path an **orbit.**

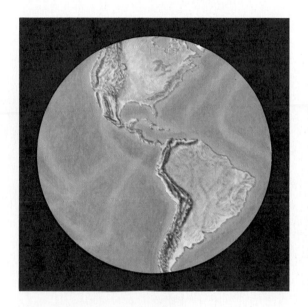

Think About It

Describe two ways the earth moves.

Lesson 4

What makes night and day?

Now we will fire our rocket engines and see more of the earth. We can fly around it.

Look! Half of the earth is brightly lighted, and half of it is in darkness.

It is daytime for people living in the lighted part. It is night for people in the dark part. From our spaceship, we can see where the light comes from—the sun.

Think About It

How would the earth be different without the sun?

120

Activity

Observe a model of night and day.

Step 1 Look at a globe. It is a model of the earth. Put a small paper person on the spot where you live.

Step 2 Observe the globe in a dark room. Step away from the globe, and shine a flashlight on it.

Step 3 Turn the globe to show day and night for the paper person.

Think About It

1. How much of the globe is lighted by the flashlight?
2. Where is it daytime on the globe? Where is it night?

Do You Know ...
The Sun Is a Star!

The sun is huge—about a million times bigger than the earth. But the sun is a medium size for a star. Many other stars are larger than the sun. They look tiny only because they are so far away.

The sun looks like a ball of fire. Stars are made of gases. The gases are so hot they glow.

The sun is our closest star. It gives us the light and heat we need to live on earth.

Tie It Together

1. Draw pictures of the earth and sun.

2. Show where it is daytime on the earth.

3. Show where it is night on the earth.

4. Tell how the earth moves.

Science Words
model
orbit

Chapter 12
The Moon

Lesson 1

Compare the moon and earth.

Now we will visit our closest neighbor in space—the moon! As we get near the moon, we see that it is very different from the earth. It should be fun to explore!

Get ready—we are going out of the spaceship.

Look for dust, rocks, and mountains. Are there any plants or animals? Do you see water and clouds? Find out what you can see in the sky. Find out how far you can run and jump.

Think About It

1. How are the moon and earth alike?
2. How are they different?

Lesson 2

Where does the moon move?

The moon orbits the earth. Sometimes the moon is on the side near the sun. Sometimes the moon is on the side of the earth away from the sun.

While the moon orbits the earth, the earth is moving around the sun. The earth and moon orbit the sun together.

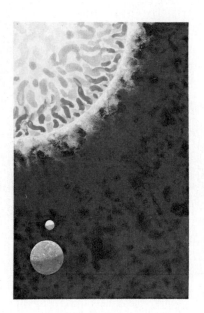 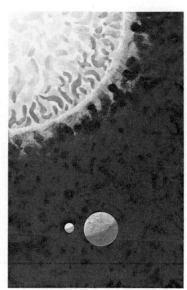 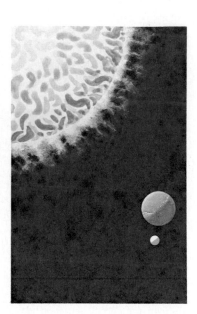

Think About It

Describe where the moon moves.

Do You Know ...

Where Does the Moon Get
Its Light?

The moon has no light of
its own. It is not hot. It does
not glow like the sun and
other stars. Moonlight
comes from the sun!

The sun shines on the
moon, just as it shines on
the earth. Part of the bright
sunlight bounces off the
moon. We can see this light
in the night sky.

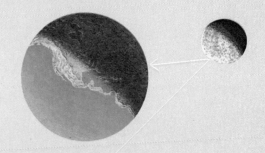

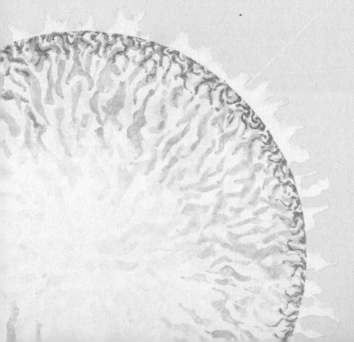

Activity

Make a moon calendar.

Step 1 Look for the moon each morning, afternoon, and night. Notice the shape of the part you can see.

Step 2 Draw this shape in a box on your calendar.

Step 3 See how many different shapes you can find in a month.

S	M	T	W	T	F	S
					1)	2
3	4	5	6	7	8	9
10	11	12	13	14	15	16
17	18	19	20	21	22	23
24	25	26	27	28	29	30
31						

Think About It

Where is the dark part of the moon?

128

Tie It Together

It is time to go home! Answer these riddles on your trip back to earth.

1. I am round like a ball. I have land and water. I have clouds and air. Plants and animals live on me. What am I?

2. I am round like a ball. I have rocks and mountains. I have no water or air. No plants or animals live on me. I am the earth's closest neighbor in space. What am I?

3. The moon orbits the earth. Together, the earth and moon go around me. What am I?

Careers
Astronomers

Astronomers can learn about space without ever leaving the earth!

They use many kinds of telescopes. Some telescopes are so large they need their own special building, called an observatory.

Astronomers measure how bright the stars are and how far away they are. Because of their work, we know a lot about outer space.

On Your Own

1. Make models of the earth, moon, and sun. Use clay, or draw them on paper. Make the sun as big as a grapefruit. Make the earth the size of a pinhead. Make the moon even smaller than a pinhead!

2. Write a story about a trip into space. Describe where you went. Draw pictures to show what it was like.

3. Find out how late you can still see the sun. Record the time. Look again next month. See if the time is earlier or later.

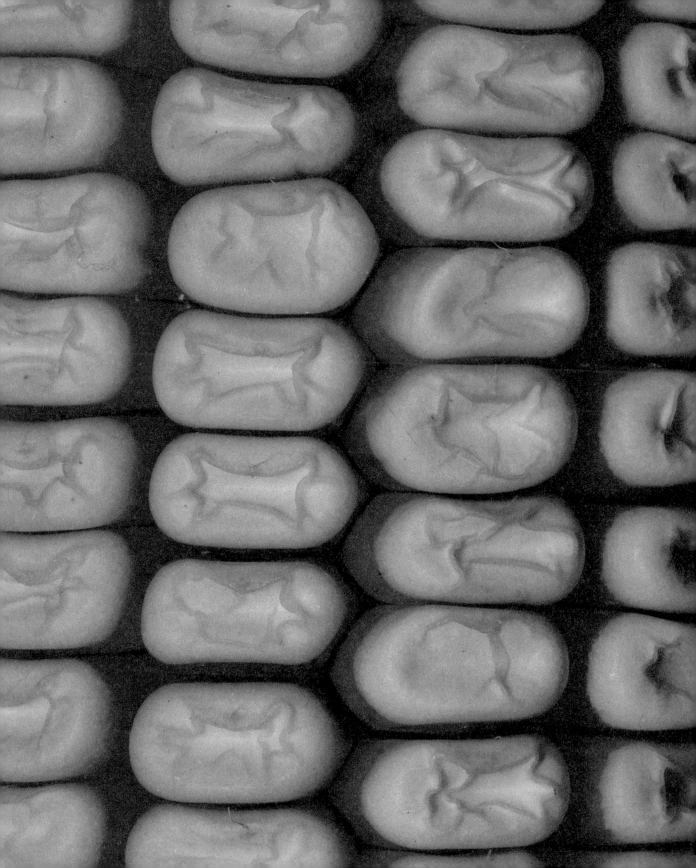

UNIT SEVEN
PLANTS

I like to plant seeds
And I like to pull
   up weeds.
Corn, tomatoes, and
   peas are neat
I am healthy
   when I eat.

Dennis Hrbek *age 7*

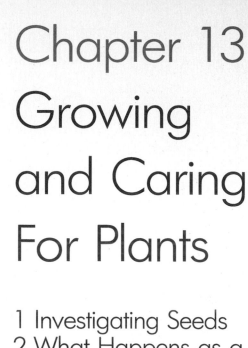

Chapter 13
Growing and Caring For Plants

1 Investigating Seeds
2 What Happens as a Seed Grows?
3 What Do Plants Need to Live and Grow?

Lesson 1
Investigate seeds.

Put seeds in four bags.
Keep one bag damp and cool.
Keep one bag damp and warm.
Keep one bag dry and cool.
Keep one bag dry and warm.

Observe the seeds every day.
Look for changes in their sizes
and shapes.

Think About It
Which seeds grew the most?

damp and cool

damp and warm

dry and cool

dry and warm

Lesson 2
What happens as a seed grows?

A very small plant is inside a seed. The plant begins to grow if it has water and the right temperature.

Roots grow down into the soil. Stems poke up through the soil. Leaves and flowers begin to form.

All the parts start from the same place—the seed!

Think About It

Describe how seeds grow.

Lesson 3

What do plants need to live and grow?

All living things need food. Green plants can make their own food. They use water, air, and sunlight to make the food.

Plants must have enough space to get the water, air, and light they need.

Soil is important for most plants. It holds a plant in place. It also holds water the plant can use.

Do all plants need the same things?

Some plants need a lot of water. They grow well in places where it rains often.

Other plants grow where very little rain falls. They store the water they get inside thick stems.

Some plants can grow underwater.

All green plants need light, air, and water. But they need different amounts of these things.

Think About It

1. Name things plants need to live and grow.
2. How can some plants live in a desert?

Activity

Record plant growth.

Step 1 Take care of two different plants. Observe them each day as they grow.

Step 2 Measure your plants every third day. Cut strips of paper as tall as your plants.

Step 3 Glue the paper strips for each plant in a row. The strips show the growth of that plant.

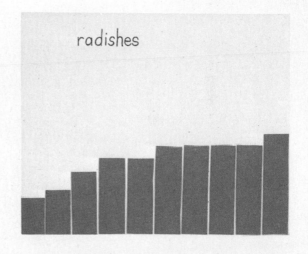

radishes

Think About It

1. Which plant grew faster?
2. How are the shapes of the two plants different?
3. Compare your own plants with those of your classmates.

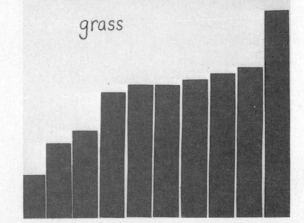

grass

141

Do You Know...
Tree Trunks Tell a Story!

When a tree is cut down, you can see many rings inside the trunk.

You can find out how old the tree was—just count the rings. Each ring shows how much the tree grew in one year.

Notice that some rings are thicker than others. The tree grew more in those years. Perhaps it rained a lot. Or maybe other trees were cut down, giving this tree more space and light.

Next time you find a tree stump, look at the growth record inside.

Tie It Together

1. Draw these pictures in the right order to show how a seed grows.

  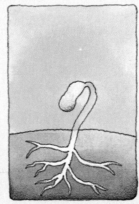 

2. Describe what you would do to help this plant grow. Tell why you think this care might help.

Chapter 14
Plant Parts

Lesson 1

Observe these parts of plants. Notice their shapes and colors.

Find the plants these parts came from.

Think About It

What properties helped you match the part with its plant?

Lesson 2

What does each part of a plant do?

Roots hold plants in the ground. They take in water from the soil.

Stems hold a plant up. They carry water from the roots to the leaves. They carry food from the leaves to other parts of the plant.

Buds are the new parts of a plant. Some buds grow into leaves and stems. Other buds become flowers.

Leaves make the food a plant needs. They use sunlight, air, and water to make the food.

New seeds form inside the plant's flowers. A fruit forms around the seeds. You might know what plant these parts came from.

How do the plant parts fit together?

Each part of an orange tree has a special job. All the parts are needed for a plant to live and grow.

Think About It

1. Which part makes food for the plant?
2. Which part is under the ground?
3. Name one place water travels inside the plant.

Activity

Observe some buds!

Step 1 Place a branch in water.

Step 2 Observe the buds every day.

Step 3 Describe the changes you see.

Think About It

1. What changes did you observe in the buds?
2. What would happen to the buds if the branches were not kept in water?

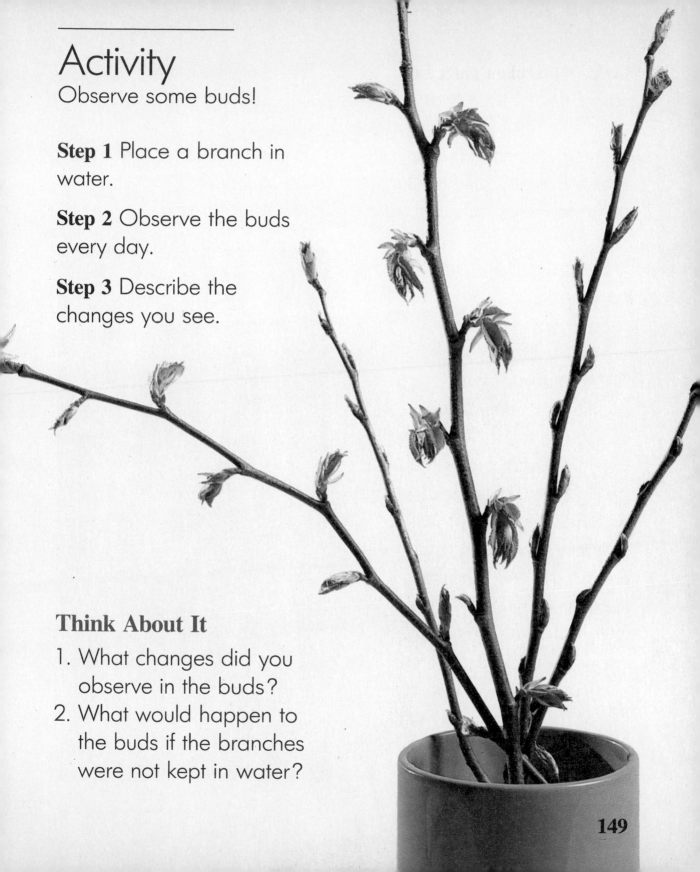

Do You Know...
Some Trees Have Many Trunks!

This picture looks like a forest. But all these trunks come from just one banyan tree.

Birds eat fruit from banyan trees. Sometimes the seeds drop into the branches of palm trees.

If a banyan seed sprouts, branches begin to form along the top of the palm tree. The banyan branches get heavy. They send shoots down to the ground.

These banyan shoots take root in the soil. They grow thick and become trunks. More and more new trunks grow to hold up the spreading banyan branches. Then no space is left in the middle for the palm tree that once held the banyan seed.

Banyan trees grow in India. A big one may have hundreds of trunks!

Tie It Together

1. I make food for the plant. I use water, air, and sunlight. What am I?

2. I carry water from the roots to the leaves. I carry food from the leaves to other plant parts. What am I?

3. You might not see me. I stay underground. I take in water for the plant. What am I?

4. I make new seeds and the fruit around the seeds. What am I?

5. We are the new parts of a plant. Some of us grow into leaves or stems. Some of us become flowers. What are we?

Science Word
bud

Careers

Farmers

Farmers work hard on a big farm. They choose seeds that can grow on their land. They plant the seeds when the temperature is right. They try to protect their crops from insects and disease.

Weather is important to farmers. Crops need water. But too much rain can hurt fruit, vegetables, and grains. Very hot or cold weather can also hurt the plants.

Sometimes the weather is just right. Then the farmer might get a big crop!

On Your Own

1. Plant some seeds. Look on the seed package to find out how much water and sunlight the plants need. Take care of your plants, and watch them grow!

2. Find out if there is a farm, greenhouse, or nature preserve that you can visit. Ask about some of the unusual plants there.

3. Observe three different plants. Compare their stems and leaves. Draw pictures of any buds, fruits, or flowers you see.

UNIT EIGHT HABITATS AND HOMES

Hippopotamus
He lives in water.
He is cooling off.
It feels cool,
 good, wet.

Mae Conde *age 8*

Chapter 15
Habitats

Lesson 1

Investigate pond water!

Some living things are very small. A hand lens can help you see them better. You can find many things living in just one bucket of pond water.

Draw a picture of a pond. Draw some living things in your picture.

Think About It

Name some living things you have seen in or near water.

Lesson 2

What lives in water?

Some living things always stay in the water. They get air from the water. They find food in the water.

A **habitat** is the place where plants and animals live. Ponds, lakes, and rivers are some water habitats. The living things in the picture are found in a lake habitat.

Oceans are another water habitat. This ocean habitat has many kinds of living things.

Think About It

Name four different water habitats.

Lesson 3

What lives near water?

Many kinds of animals live close to water. Here they find plenty of food and places to hide.

You could find these animals in a **wetland** habitat. A wetland is soaked with water most of the time. Swamps and marshes are some kinds of wetlands.

Think About It

Name two reasons animals live near water.

Activity

Find the animals in the wetland habitat.

1. These animals spend much of their lives on land, but they lay eggs in water.

2. These animals can swim in water, but they lay eggs on land.

3. The heron and raccoon eat fish and crayfish that live in water.

Think About It

Describe what each animal does on land and in water.

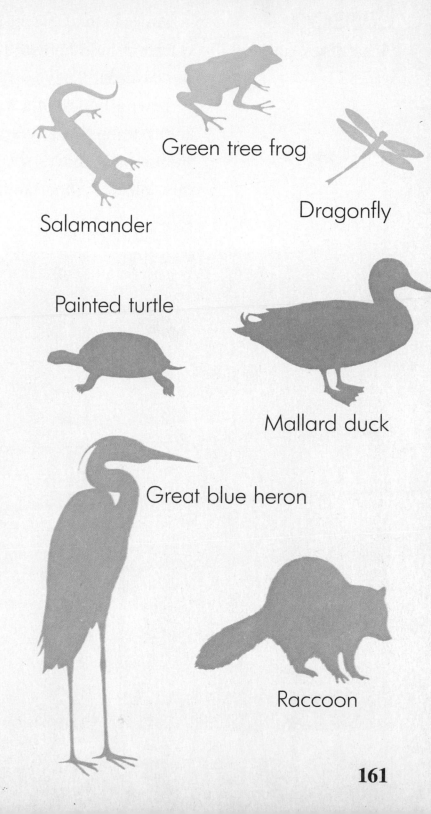

Salamander

Green tree frog

Dragonfly

Painted turtle

Mallard duck

Great blue heron

Raccoon

Lesson 4
What lives on land?

Animals and plants live together in many different land habitats. Land habitats can be hot or cold. They can be wet or dry.

Living things in a habitat need other living things. Many animals eat plants. As the animals move, seeds get scattered to new places. Some animals eat insects or other animals.

Some plants make good homes for animals. Even the shade from plants can be a place to rest.

Think About It

How could land animals use plants in a hot place and in a cold place?

Do You Know...
Some Animals Change Habitats!

Some habitats become very cold in winter. The animals may move—or migrate—to a warmer place.

Monarch butterflies migrate. Some spend the winter in California or Florida.

Millions of monarchs fly to one place in the mountains of Mexico. The resting butterflies can cover up whole trees there!

One by one, the monarchs return north in the spring to lay their eggs.

Tie It Together

1. Describe a habitat for each of these living things.

2. What animals might live here? What could they use for food?

Science Words
habitat
wetland

Chapter 16
Homes

Lesson 1

Draw plans for a home!

Many animals build homes. They sleep, store food, and protect their young in these homes.

You need a home too. List the things you need to live. Then, draw plans for your home. Make it just right for you!

Think About It

Compare your own plans with the plans of a classmate.

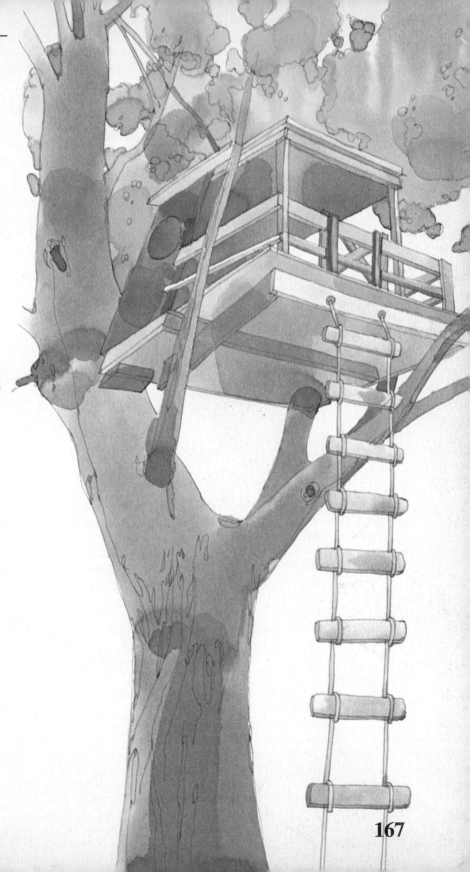

167

Lesson 2

What kinds of homes do animals build?

A **nest** is a special place made for eggs and young animals. Nests come in many shapes and sizes.

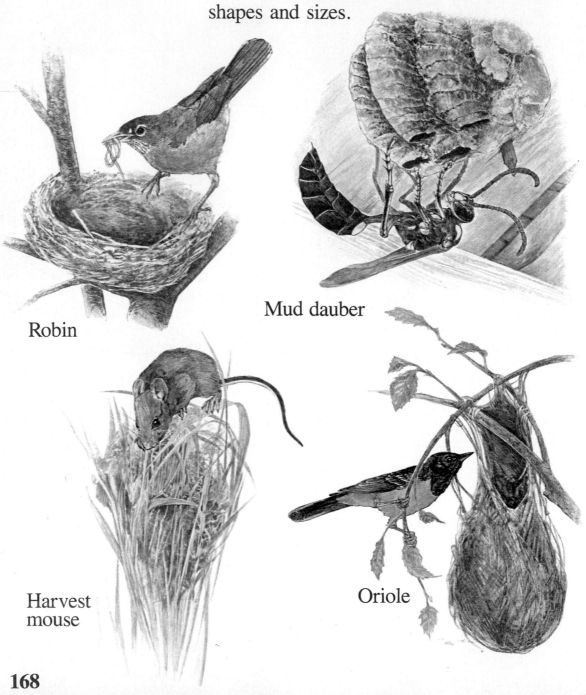

Robin

Mud dauber

Harvest
mouse

Oriole

Alligator

Horned grebe

Animals use what they find in their habitats to build homes. Some animals make nests out of twigs, grass, leaves, and mud.

Stickleback

What are some underground homes?

Gophers and prairie dogs dig—or **burrow**—under the ground. These prairie dogs built their own city!

Beavers build their homes from sticks and mud. To get inside, the beavers swim through underwater tunnels.

Think About It

What animal nests and homes have you seen?

170

Imagine ...

You Could Visit an Ant's Home!

Ants work together to make a home. Some ants dig tunnels. They can make rooms in an old log, under a rock, or down in the ground. A hill of dirt or sand may mark the opening to the home.

It is dark inside the ant's home. Ants cannot see in the dark. They find their way by touch and smell.

Pretend you are an ant. Use your imagination to take a trip into the ant's home.

Describe each place marked by a letter on the picture. What could you feel or smell? What could you hear?

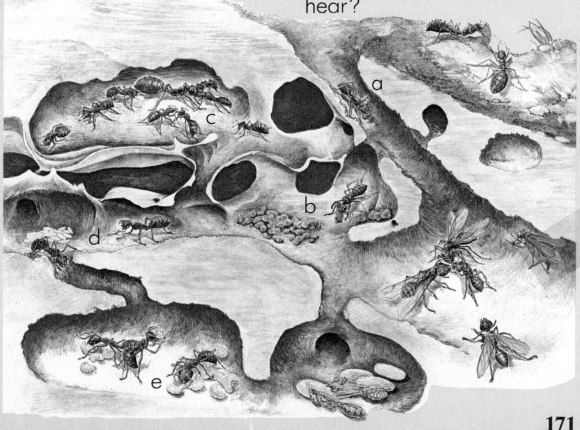

Activity
Build a nest!

Step 1 Look at pictures of different nests. Choose the kind you would like to make.

Step 2 Get materials an animal might find in its habitat.

Step 3 Use the materials to make a nest.

Think About It

What animal might have the kind of nest you made?

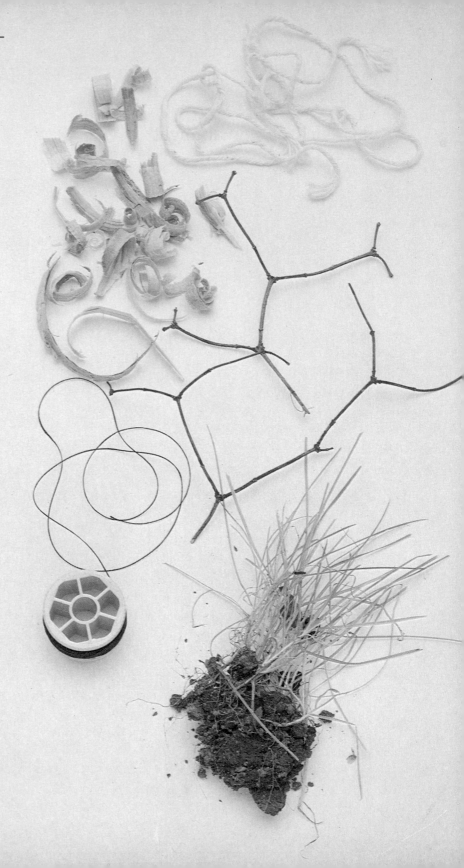

Tie It Together

1. What kind of animal might live in each home?

2. Name ways the animals would use these homes.

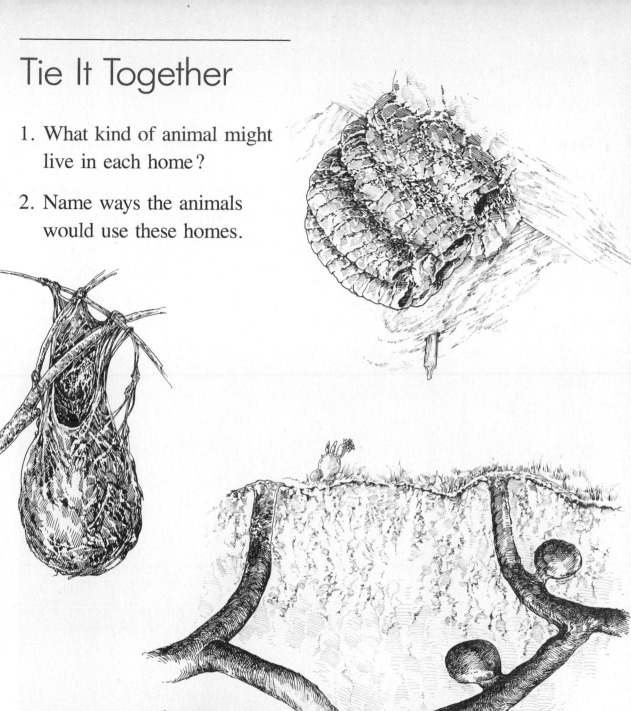

Science Words
nest
burrow

Careers
Marine Biologists

A marine biologist studies ocean life and habitats. Some marine biologists dive under the water to learn about living things in their habitats.

The biologists in the picture can stay underwater for a long time. They write about what they observe. They might bring some water life to a lab for more study.

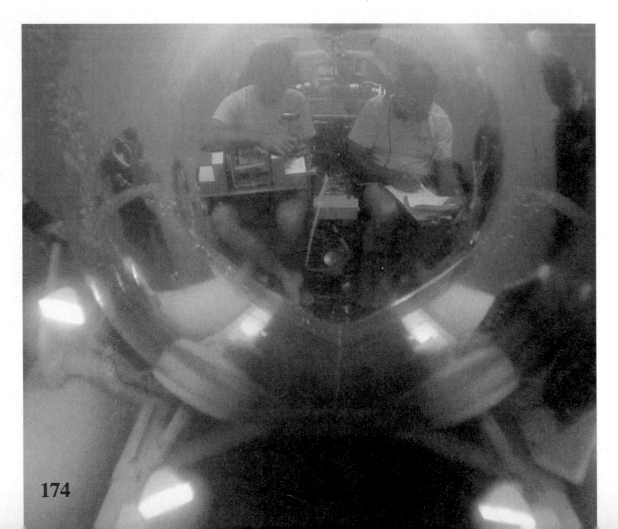

On Your Own

1. Cut off one side of a shoe box. Draw or paint a wetland habitat inside. Glue grass and leaves inside for some plant life. Make models of wetland animals from clay or paper.

2. Go on a hike. Look for some plant or animal. As you walk, find other places with the same kind of living thing. Describe its habitat.

3. Read a story about an animal you like. Find out what kind of home it has. Draw the animal in its home.

Glossary/Index

adult, page 31: grown-up.
Some young animals change a lot before they become adults.

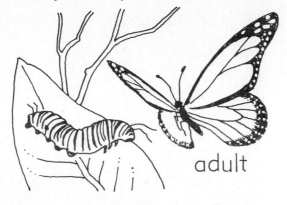
adult

blood, page 16: the red liquid that goes through all parts of your body.

bone, page 14: one of the hard pieces inside that gives your body its shape.

bud, page 147: the new part of a plant that may become a leaf, stem, or flower.
You can find many buds on plants in spring.

burrow, page 170: dig a hole under the ground.
Gophers burrow to make their homes. Prairie dogs also live in burrows.

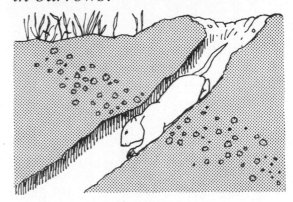

compare, page 29: find out how two things are alike or different.
Compare the shape of the ball with the shape of the bat.

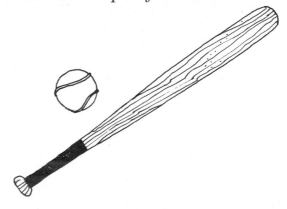

expand, page 84: grow larger and take up more space.
A balloon expands when you blow it up.

flow, page 53: pour out in an even stream.
All liquids flow.

force, page 102: a push or a pull.
It takes more force to roll a bowling ball than to roll a marble.

friction, page 96: a force that makes it harder to slide objects back and forth.
Friction made the wagon stop rolling on the bumpy road.

gas, page 54: matter that spreads out to fill its container.
Air is made of gases.

habitat, page 158: the place where a plant or animal lives.
Many animals live in a water habitat.

177

hatch, page 31: come out of an egg.
A chick hatches about 21 days after the egg is laid.

heart, page 16: the part of your body that pumps blood.

investigate, page 61: find out about something by doing things and observing what happens.
You must investigate to see if an object floats.

invisible, page 54: cannot be seen.
Many gases, such as air, are invisible.

joint, page 14: the place where two bones fit together.
Elbows and knees are joints.

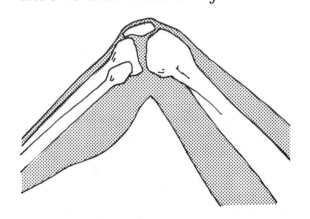

lay, page 31: bring forth eggs.
Birds and turtles lay eggs.

liquid, page 53: matter that flows and takes the shape of its container.
Water is a liquid when you can pour it.

matter, page 52: anything that takes up space.
Solids, liquids, and gases are three kinds of matter.

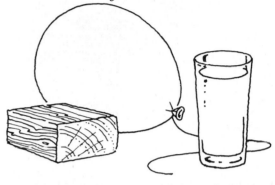

lungs, page 16: parts of your body that take in air.

machine, page 106: something that helps you do a job faster and easier.

measure, page 8: find the size of something.

model, page 115: a copy of something real.
It is fun to build a model car.

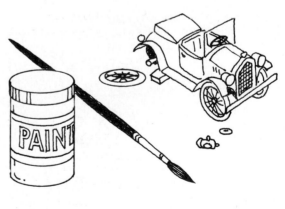

motion, page 94: moving from place to place.
A falling leaf is in motion.

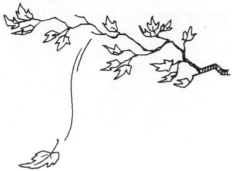

muscle, page 15: the part of your body attached to the bones that helps you move.

nest, page 168: something built by animals to hold eggs or young animals.

observe, page 6: look carefully, using any or all of your senses.

orbit, page 119: the path an object makes when it goes around something in space.

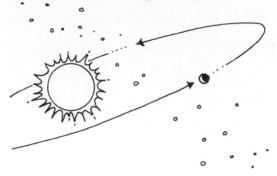

plant parts, page 136: roots, stems, leaves, and flowers.

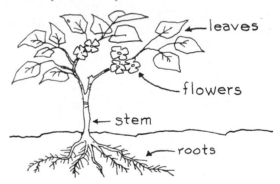

predict, page 63: use what you know to say what you think will happen next.
When you see dark clouds and lightning, you might predict there will be rain.

property, page 51: word that describes what something is like.
Cold and hard are two properties of ice.

solid, page 52: matter that has a shape of its own.
Water is a solid when it is frozen into an ice cube.

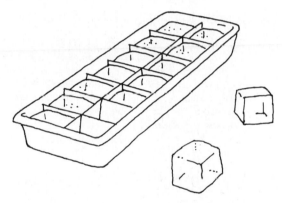

stomach, page 17: a part of your body that breaks down food.

tadpole, page 34: a very young frog or toad.
Tadpoles have long tails and must stay in water.

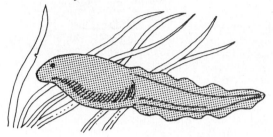

temperature, page 82: the measure of how hot something is.
What is the temperature outside today?

thermometer, page 82: tool that measures exactly how hot an object is.

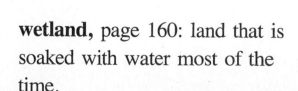

wetland, page 160: land that is soaked with water most of the time.

Acknowledgements

Positions of photographs are shown in abbreviated form as follows: top (t), bottom (b), left (l), right (r), center (c). All photographs not credited are the property of Scott, Foresman and Company. Cover, illustration by William Peterson, photograph by Rod Planck/Tom Stack & Assoc.; 2, DPI; 8, Ted Streshinsky; 26, Robert W. Mitchell/Animals Animals; 28, Hans Reinhard/Bruce Coleman Ltd.; 29, (tl) Jeff Foott; (tr) Tom Stack & Assoc.; (cl) E.R. Degginger; (cr) E.R. Degginger. (b) Salvatore Giordano III; 30, (t) David G. Wacker/Tom Stack & Assoc.; (bl) David R. Frazier; (br) Hans Reinhard/Bruce Coleman Ltd.; 31, (t) Ron Dillon/Tom Stack & Assoc.; (c) E.R. Degginger; (b) Jane Burton/Bruce Coleman Ltd.; 32, Kathy and Alan Linn; 33, (t) Kathy and Alan Linn; (c) Breck P. Kent; (bl), E.R. Degginger; (br) Sdeuard C. Bisserot; 36, H. Rivarola/Bruce Coleman Ltd.; 37, (t) Bob & Clara Calhoun/Bruce Coleman Ltd.; (c) Jane Burton/Bruce Coleman Ltd.; (bl) William H. Allen, Jr.; (br) Anthony Bannister/N.H.P.A.; 40, (t) Jane Burton/Bruce Coleman Ltd.; (l) E.R. Degginger; (b) M. Werner/Tom Stack & Assoc.; 41, (tl) M. Claye/Jacana; (tr) Walter Chandoha; (bl) Gerald Cubitt/Bruce Coleman Ltd.; (br) John Lythgoe/Seaphot; 42, (l) Alan Root/Bruce Coleman Ltd.; (r) Jean-Paul Ferrero/Ardea London; 43, (tl) Stephan Dalton/N.H.P.A., (r) Jack F. Dermid; (bl) Herve Chaumeton/Jacana; 45, (t) Joe B. Blossom/N.H.P.A.; (c) Ardea London; (b) Pat Morris/Ardea London; 46, Michael Heron/Woodfin Camp & Assoc.; 48, Thomas Ives; 58, From *Bartholomew and the Oobleck*, by Dr. Seuss. Copyright 1949 by Dr. Seuss. Reprinted by permission of Random House, Inc.; 68, E.A. Janes/N.H.P.A.; 70, Stockphotos, Inc.; 72, Howard Sochurek; 77, Stephan Collins/Photo Researchers; 88, Robert C. King; 90, Bruce Curtis/Peter Arnold, Inc.; 100, Robert Isear/DPI; 110, David Burnett/Contact Press Images; 112, NASA; 114, NASA; 116 (t) Grant Heilman; (c) Chuck Fishman/DPI; (b) NASA; 117, NASA; 122, Harald Sund; 124, NASA; 125, NASA; 130, Dan McCoy/Rainbow; 132, Robert P. Carr/Bruce Coleman Inc.; 136, Herve Chaumeton; 139, (l) Errath/Explorer; (r) Walter Chandoha; 140, (t) Kjell B. Sandved/Bruce Coleman Inc.; (c) Harald Sund; 150, Phil & Loretta Hermann; 152, J. Gordon Miller/Shostal; 154, Giuseppe Mazza; 156, Thomas Hollyman/Photo Researchers; 157, (t) William H. Amos/Bruce Coleman Inc.; (c) E.R. Degginger; (b) Z. Leszczynski from Breck P. Kent; 162 (l) Bruce Coleman Ltd.; (r) Breck P. Kent; 163 (l) Leonard Lee Rue III/DPI; (r) Shelly Grossman/Woodfin Camp & Assoc.; 164, Jeff Foott/Bruce Coleman Inc.; 165, Ed Cooper; 166, Harry Engels/Photo Researchers; 174, Flip Schulke/Seaphot.

Edward Hughes: design implementation, internal art and photographic direction.

We wish to express our appreciation to the following schools for their contributions:

Poems for the series were written by children at Fairfield Public Schools, Fairfield, Connecticut; Greeley School, Winnetka, Illinois; Howland School, Chicago, Illinois; Indian Oasis Elementary District, Sells, Arizona; and Model Laboratory School, Eastern Kentucky University, Richmond, Kentucky.

Cloze reading tests for the series were administered at Banting Elementary School, Waukesha, Wisconsin; and Gospel Lutheran Grade School, Milwaukee, Wisconsin.

Photographs for Book 2 were taken at Orrington School, Evanston, Illinois.